TOM NESTOR
DRIVING WITH DAISY

A regular columnist with the *Limerick Leader* for
many years, Tom Nestor is author of the acclaimed
memoir *The Keeper of Absalom's Island*. He has also
written plays for RTÉ and BBC, and has had
numerous short stories and a novel published.

NEW ISLAND *Open Door*

DRIVING WITH DAISY
First published January 2002
by New Island
2 Brookside
Dundrum Road
Dublin 14

www.newisland.ie

A CIP catalogue record for this book is available from the British Library

ISBN 1 902602 71 4

New Island Books receives financial assistance from
The Arts Council (An Chomhairle Ealaíon), Dublin, Ireland.

Typeset by New Island
Printed in Ireland by ColourBooks
Cover design by Artmark

1 3 5 4 2

NEW ISLAND *Open Door*

Welcome to the third Open Door series. Once again, some of Ireland's best-loved authors have come up with a wonderful array of books for this unique series. Branching out for the first time into non-fiction, Tom Nestor's warm and moving childhood memoir will ring bells with many who grew up in 1940s' rural Ireland, while Margaret Neylon introduces us to the secret of numbers, or 'numerology', and invites us to have a look at what's in store in our lives. Add to this four diverse stories from best-selling authors Maeve Binchy, Vincent Banville, Cathy Kelly and Deirdre Purcell — from family feud and the bloom of late romance, to crime-solving on Dublin's mean streets and unravelling secrets and lies inside a family home — and you will find something here to suit everyone's taste. And, like all good stories, we hope these books will open doors — of the imagination and of opportunity — for adult readers of all ages.

All royalties from the Irish sales of the Open Door series go to a charity of the author's choice. *Driving With Daisy* royalties go to St Vincent de Paul, Birr, Co. Offaly.

THE OPEN DOOR SERIES IS DEVELOPED WITH THE ASSISTANCE OF THE CITY OF DUBLIN VOCATIONAL EDUCATION COMMITTEE.

Dear Reader,

On behalf of myself and the other contributing authors, I would like to welcome you to the third Open Door series. We hope that you enjoy the books and that reading becomes a lasting pleasure in your life.

Warmest wishes,

Patricia Scanlan.

Patricia Scanlan
Series Editor

To May

During the time of the Second World War and for some years after that, food was scarce. At that time we only went to the town of Rath when we needed new clothing or when some broken piece of farm machinery had to be fixed. Everything else we bought in Tommy Hanley's shop in Creeves. It was a couple of miles away, about half the distance to Rath. A person could buy most things there: groceries, hardware, animal feed, twine, coal. 'Almost everything from a needle to an anchor,' his trade slogan read. It was written in a brass plate beside the entrance door. If he didn't have something, he would order it down from Dublin or out from Limerick. It made the item sound very rare and important.

Dublin was so far away it might as well have been in another country. Limerick was a city that made our rural village sound like a backwater.

When we needed something from Hanley's our neighbour Pat the Dog would fetch it. We called him Pat the Dog because that was a saying of his. Instead of saying 'cool down' when someone got upset and angry, he would say, 'pat the dog'. He cycled home from work on a Friday night like a laden camel. There was an oilskin bag hanging from each side of the handlebars. There was a larger one dangling from the bar. The carrier was so full that it was falling over the side. I can see him battling against the wind and the bike wobbling as he came up the hill by Mick Smith's cottage.

When the war ended, word reached us about the wonderful things that had reached the shops in Rath. My older sisters, wiser and more in tune with the outside world, had heard that there were oranges and bananas arriving in Dublin. It was only a matter of time before they found their way to our neck of the woods. But wonderful as these fruits were, they were nothing compared to chocolate. It melted on the tongue and gave a pleasure that was hard to describe. Listening to them, I saw Rath as a kind of caravan stop where traders brought magical gifts from a land of spices on the far side of the world.

When I was eleven and we had a little more money to spend, I became the messenger boy. Every Saturday morning I set out for Rath. It was five and a half miles away and I did most of the journey on foot. There was only one bicycle in our house, which my eldest brother had wrecked. The pedals were worn down. There were no brakes. The front wheel was more square than round and the handlebars had been twisted out of shape.

In the beginning, I looked forward to those trips. I set off with an oilskin message bag and my mother's message list pinned to the lining of my jacket. I saw myself as a kind of pioneer. I was heading into unknown territory, not knowing what adventures I might find on the way. I would meet buffalo and coyotes, silver fox and grizzly bear. Perhaps the Indians would be raiding out of the forests in the Massey estate.

Paddy White, who worked on

Colonel Cripps's stud farm, was responsible for putting those kind of ideas into my head. He let me read the Western books that the Colonel loaned to him. My mind was a whirl of sounds and smells, of mesas, prairie and heather. I believed those stories. I thought the cowboy was as natural a part of America as the farmer was of mine. I thought all Indians were savages and that all white pioneers were perfect Christians. Like the white missionaries who went from Ireland to Africa, they spoke the true word of God against the evil works of the devil.

After a few Saturdays my journey became known. Children kept watch for me behind windows and half-closed doors. I was a God-sent messenger who went to Rath every Saturday, along a route that no one had travelled much before, except the Marshall.

McMahon's first name was Jim but he was called Marshall after Napoleon's military hero. Once a week, with a full cart, he came out from the boglands around his home and sold peat from door to door in Rath. As he journeyed to the town, people came out of their houses, not to buy his turf but to ask him to do messages for them. He obliged and they wanted more. They blamed him for the poor quality of the goods he brought, queried the change and were angry with him if he forgot. So he stopped serving. He sat up there in the high seat that jutted out from the creel of turf. He greeted everyone he passed with the civil salute and a shake of his head. Every time they asked him, he had the same answer: 'Don't do no messages for no one no more.'

I would have loved to give the

Marshall's answer to Mrs Mack. Hers was the first house I passed on my way and she was waiting from the moment I came on to the road at the end of our lane. She had a tongue like a rasp and a war in her mind about the unfairness of the world she had been cast into. Poor as she made herself out to be, she would have the price of half-a-dozen lamb chops, which we could never afford then. I got the money for the meat wrapped up in one piece of paper. As I tried to walk away she grabbed me by the shoulder and gave me another piece. The second roll of paper had more money and a list of horse names. I was to go to the clerk in the bookmaker's shop and have him transfer them onto a betting slip. If I wasn't allowed near the counter, she told me, I was to wait until some adult I knew and could trust came along and would place the bet for me. Innocent as I was and afraid of her tongue, I accepted it. She knew exactly what her winnings would be if either of the wagers came good.

I dealt with Mrs Mack by taking another route across the fields. It brought me out at White's Cross, a hundred yards beyond her house. Beyond the cross I would come upon the Harolds, father and son. For years they had lived without a woman in the house and each had almost become a copy of the other. Jimmy was thirty years younger than his father, and the only difference I could see was that one face looked older. They spoke the same words in the same accent.

Both were very shy and would choose to avoid people as far as possible. My father said that they owned one pipe. Most of the talk that passed between them was an argument about its use. Years later, when the father had passed on, I came across Jimmy one day cutting thistles in a field. He was singing and I was amazed as I listened. Not only could Jimmy sing very well, but the song he was singing was as much out of place as if he were singing an operatic aria.

'I have heard the mavis singing her love song to the morn,
I have seen the dew drop clinging to the rose just newly born.'

As he sang I wondered how something beautiful could suddenly appear in the most unlikely place. The moment Jimmy realised I was there, the singing stopped in a sudden gasp, and a little pale shadow of shyness crept over his sun-tanned face. They were a twin puzzle, father and son. They showed nothing of themselves to their neighbours, no clues to discover what their world was like. We knew nothing about their personalities.

Once, my cousin Con and I were sneaking along by the hedgerow, with Con's new air gun. We were looking for a magpie that had stolen eggs from a nearby nest. At the far side of the hedge, the elder Harold was loading hay onto a cart. It was a humid evening and the midges were swarming in waves in the shelter of the hedge. We poked the air gun through the hedge and fired at the fleshy part of the horse's hindquarter. The elder Harold took little notice when the horse reacted to the first pellet. But when we had fired some more and the horse was plunging between the shafts, the old man thumped his head as if he couldn't believe what he was seeing. He took off his hat and bent to beat off the invisible horseflies. He searched under the neck collar for something that might be biting the horse's flesh. He stood with his hands on his hips, disbelief all over his face. His calm fifteen-year-old horse was behaving like a stabled stallion on a diet of oats. Then he took off his hat, crossed himself and said a prayer.

Everyone who passed the Harold house was noticed. There was a high wall in front and the passer-by would only be visible for a few moments. But they never missed the shadow of somebody going by the gate. When I looked back, I would surprise the son or the father peeping round. The face alone would be visible and it would duck out of sight when I looked.

A hundred yards from the Harold house there was a quarry. In the heel of one Sunday evening when I was nearing my ninth birthday, I chased in there hunting a rabbit. I was alone except for the dogs. There was a ledge jutting out from the rock. Underneath the ledge lay a man and woman. They were making love. The man I knew well. He was a neighbour, with a wife and several children. I knew that the woman lying with the man was not his wife. I stood there in shock until then the man lifted his head and looked at me. He mouthed a couple of swear words and made a rude sign with his fingers.

I whistled up the dogs but lost all interest in the hunt. It wasn't finding the couple in the lovemaking act that shocked me. Neither was it the fact that I knew the man to be a regular churchgoer and a friend of the priest. What bothered me was that I knew then the truth of something I'd had my doubts about. The mystery of birth was explained. The stories about storks that left baby parcels on doorsteps were all fairytales. I had my suspicions all along. I had grown up surrounded by animals and had watched their goings on. I knew where young animals came from. It was all plain now, the man and the woman, the cow and the bull. There was no mystery, no magic.

I was into a loping canter by the time I reached Ned Wall's house, because I was afraid. The thatched house was hidden by a hedge and a huge lilac. Both had grown out of control and were spreading along the north gable. It was like a cottage from an English rural landscape painting. Some years ago, a splinter had entered Ned's eye as he was chopping firewood. He had neglected it and the sore had turned to poison.

One summer's evening, when we mowed the meadow opposite Ned Wall's house, my uncle Lara sent me in for a drink of water. Ned Wall was sitting in the gloom at the fireside and smoke was floating around the room. Everywhere was smoked: the walls, the chair backs, the small windowpanes. The chimney-breast had turned brown and wrinkled like old paper. But it was the sight of Ned Wall in his backless chair by the fire that set my heart racing and filled my nights with devils and monsters. His hands and the good side of his face were smoked like the side of bacon that hung on our kitchen wall. Around him the smoke spun, and out from the smog this terrible face turned to look at me. One side of it had rotted away.

Ned Wall used to play the flute. He played traditional music, mostly slow airs. It was unusual because there was little traditional culture in the place where we lived. The fact was that we looked down on those values, as did the people a hundred years before when they were moving away from the Irish language. In people's minds, native music and dance were linked to poverty and slavery. I remember an aunt telling my mother about a dance she had been to. It was a *céilí*, an Irish word for the Irish way of dancing. She spoke with scorn about the sweat-filled room, the basic steps, the wild whoops and, above all, the thunder of hobnailed boots on the floor when the dance ended.

I listened to Ned Wall's slow airs on summer evenings. He brought the chair to the flagstone by the road and played in the great stillness. There was a haunting loveliness to the 'Lament for Staker Wallis', as there was to Jim Harold's 'Annie Laurie'. I heard snatches of it in my sleep. It followed me by day and I heard it in the quiet of fields and the shelter of hedges. I heard it when I was far away and it made me long for the sounds and the warmth of home. It reminded me of the blackbird that sang in the apple tree in our orchard. It seemed to tell us that it was the only singing bird in the world so gifted.

There is no evidence now of Wall's cottage. Nothing to show that a house once stood there, and that a man with a rotting face played haunting music in the stillness of an evening. Twenty-five years ago, my wife May and I searched amid the briars and the wild hedge until we had found the stunted lilac. An offspring from it now grows in our back garden. It is always slow to flower and quick to shed. We suffer it only because of its links to a distant past. Sometimes, in the early fall of twilight, I think I hear music from the corner where it grows.

★

I ran past Tom Flavin's house. It was thatched like ours but there was no door on the side that faced the road. I had visited there once, delivering pork steak and black puddings, and they had kept me for tea. The house was full of adults and the conversation full of child talk. A sister passed a slice of bread to a big well-built brother.

'There now, pettens. Say who's good to Jimmy?'

'My little Lena is. My own lil' Lena is good to Jimmy.'

The Flavin family and ours had once pooled labour. Two rows of potatoes had been planted when the call came for dinner. The seed was shining in the sun, waiting for its cover of farmyard manure and soil. The eldest Flavin stood on the headland with his hands on his hips, looking back at the morning's work.

'If they come,' he said, 'they won't come, and if they won't come, they'll come.'

His neighbours thought he spoke in riddles. And so he did because old man Flavin spoke in a complicated way. But my father liked such variations and he would test us with that puzzle. I failed the test, as did others older than me. It was my mother who finally shone light on the puzzle, as she had done for all who had gone before me. Old man Flavin was afraid of the crows, especially the greys and the scalds. If they lighted on the field during dinner, when there was no one to shoo them away, they would eat all the uncovered potatoes.

If I had time and the weather was good, I would take to the fields opposite Flavin's and follow the journey of the stream. It had just flown gurgling under the single arch of the stone bridge. This was the same stream that sprung from a well, half a mile north of my home. It crossed the road at Whacker's and sometimes in winter and spring flooded his garden.

Whacker, who was a year older than me, had caught a trout one summer's day. He had snared it with a makeshift loop of twine worked under a stone. He brought it down in a pan and showed it to a group of us who were hurling in Dunne's field. The pan passed in wonder from hand to hand. None of us had been that close before to a creature of the water. The Whacker kept the trout imprisoned on the windowsill until he found it stiff and lifeless one day. For hours Whacker and I had rested our arms on the windowsill, marvelling at the little creature in its prison.

The stream ran by the patch of land where the cattle watered and the cows were milked. When the stream flooded and then dried up, it left a hard-baked piece of ground in summer. It looked like the picture of a watering hole in Kenya that I had seen in a religious magazine called *The Far East*. Con and I found a little silver fish stranded in a mud-pool. It was a minnow, his father told us. It led us to discover that part of the stream where the minnows lived.

There was a pair of pine logs laid side-by-side over the stream. They formed a crossing to the other bank.

Below the bridge, in the silted bed, was a shoal of little fish. We had crossed that log bridge a thousand times. We had fought duels on it, we had raced over it and lain to rest on it, and we had never seen a minnow. Now they were darting from bank to bank so swiftly that they seemed only shadows. They were sending out puffs of silt like a thousand little bombs. They were everywhere and had been invisible up to now because we didn't expect to see them. We tied lengths of cord to the necks of jam jars and trapped the fish. Hannah, Con's mother, gave us a glass bowl. As with Whacker's trout, we placed the bowl on the windowsill. Hour after hour, we watched the wonder of movement, that great miracle that nature had formed on living things.

I can still feel those times through

my senses. I feel the soothing warmth of mud through my toes. I smell watercress, and hear the clay buzz like an army of crickets as it dried beneath the sun. It was the summer of the minnows. Con and I were a pair of freckled-faced kids, sun-tanned on lower arms and below the knees. We skirted slyly by the hedgerows as we dodged the work in both our homes. I think of us as barefooted Huckleberry Finns, with glass jars slung from pieces of twine, heading for Moon River.

★

Where I came to the road again, there was a tiny thatched house built against the great wall of Mara's estate. You would never know there was a house there, if it weren't for the column of smoke, because the roof was beneath the level of the wall. This was Aggie's house. I had first seen her when she came into the aisle in the church where our family pew was. I had never seen anyone so old. She was older than Nanna, who lived in the house next door, and who scared me as she passed the kitchen window. Nanna dressed in black and seemed to have a tiny face beneath the rim of her bonnet. What I saw had the pale colour of waxed skin. When she passed the window I thought some messenger from beyond the grave was coming to take me away.

Aggie had the look of someone astray in the head and who loved every moment of it. Her hair was like a wig of sheep's wool casually laid on her head. It seemed to be in a different position each time I met her. The hair grew out of her scalp in yellow tufts.

Aggie's speech was like her hair. It came in wild spills of words followed by spells of quietness. In the silence, she looked at me with her face twisted sideways like a curious bird. It was as if she was waiting for the words she had spoken to reform and return. She cackled as much as she spoke. She would hop from one foot to the other when something struck her as funny.

I knew Aggie was harmless. My father used to say that she was as sane as the rest of us. Maybe she was because it takes a special sense to reduce one's lot to a state of comedy, to laugh at a queer old world and think it amusing. Sometimes I wondered if that was the way she had planned it, as if throwing aside normal ways was the best way to handle life.

Aggie loved to talk. She would fix her bony old fingers like a vice around my wrist and make me a prisoner of her chatter. The hens and the bantam fowl scraped and pecked in the cropped grass on the road's margin. People used to talk about how odd that was. It was madder than all things about Aggie because in front of her half-door were acres upon acres of the Mara estate. It stretched as far as the eye could see, rich and secure behind the high wall. And yet this old woman chose to feed her fowl on the public roadway and had to keep a constant watch over them. But there was method in her behaviour, for otherwise people would pass by without a word. Everyone who passed was forced to halt and listen while Aggie poured forth her strange madcap cackle.

In my mind, I twinned Aggie with Nonie, who lived in the shadow of the church. Nonie used tell me about the fairies, the little people she called them. They scampered up and down her slated roof and robbed her sleep. Con and I hid in the long grass in Lowe's meadow and threw pebbles onto the roof. Eventually her anger would outdo her dread of the fearful little ones. She would rush out from her kitchen and pour a stream of abuse upon her invisible tormentors on the roof.

There is nothing left of Aggie's house now to show that a barmy old woman had lived there. She brought me in once, a very hot day in June, as I was returning, weary and thirsty, from Rath. She wrapped her bony fingers around my wrist and shooed the hens and bantams through the gate before us. I was given a drink from a barrel with a wooden lid. The water tasted like it had come from God's own well on the very day he had made it. She poured it from a ladle into a mug that was decorated with a red stripe. There was a hint of gun-barrel blue when the water ran from the ladle. It was shot through by the glint of sun piercing the smoked glass of the window. When I left, she presented me with a dozen rabbit snares and a broken-down goldfinch cage.

'Take them away, son. Far from catching rabbits or trapping birds I be now.'

We came out to the road again where the flock of hens and bantams were squawking and fighting. The gnarled old fingers tightened on my wrist and she cocked her head.

'Whist,' she said, with a note of fear, 'is that the booze of a motor I hear?'

The old order was changing. The world was spinning on a different course, tuning to strange signals and movements. The motorcar was coming. Soon it would come by the white road and leave dust trails like a cowboy's horse. When that happened, old Aggie Butler would close the wooden gate and move her flock to the safety within. And then, until their time too came to an end, people on foot and on horse would pass by unnoticed.

I went along by the great stonewall of Mara's estate. My ancestors had built that wall. A man and his labour, his horse and his cart, were valued at the rate of three pence a day. The estate wall was the landlord's folly — a mixture of oddness and a display of rank. It wasn't built for protection because the landlord was the great power. But it shut off the manor seat from the rude gaze of lowly peasants. Every peasant outside the high wall thought it an act of nonsense because really it kept the landed set in rather than kept the landless people out. I would always hear how odd the so-called quality was. Their high stone walls, the avenues of elm, the stands of beech, the feats of horsemanship. But those things were simply distractions that kept the boredom at bay.

Those were days when the horse was king. It applied to all breeds: draught horses, plough horses, high stepping cobs, hunters and thoroughbreds. Our neighbours, the Maras and the Burys, who were cousins, rode to hounds. They visited each other often, always on horseback, passing by on the road around our land. It seemed to me that they were the winners of life and were sharing the fruits of victory. They sat above us in seats of power that raised them over the lowly. It made us wonder what turn of fate had arranged it that some people had never to work or toil as we did. They could idly ride the white roads while the rest of us were bent to our tasks.

But we never envied the horsy families. They were simply a part of God's way. In His vast wisdom he had granted a saddle to one and a shovel to another. But I admired from a distance the rank and the romance that surrounded the landed people. I saw the great men of history in the horsemen who passed our humble way. I saw the glory of empire in the fox-hunt. I saw the mark of the high born in the great houses and their ballrooms.

I probed at the outskirts of that lifestyle. I would watch for hours the cartwheel that Shaw's racehorses formed, under the shelter of the chestnut tree. Sometimes the cartwheel would break away like the Arab stallions in Duffy's circus, and go galloping headlong around the railed meadow. I had found a stirrup in our gable wall and another thrown in a hedge. I polished them till they were gleaming like silver. On the road beyond our lane, where the fox-hunt had passed, I found the broken pieces of a bridle. I repaired it and when no one was looking I fitted it to the head of our working mare. I imagined us both, she a thoroughbred and me a red-coated Master of Hounds, trotting to the meet at White's Cross.

The fox-hunt stirred my blood and lifted my heart. It did the same to most youngsters I knew and many an adult too. When we heard the hounds and the distant bugle sound, Miss Abigail, our school teacher, would let us follow the hunt. We chased all day, opening gates for aged riders and handsome women. A man with a red face and a gold pin in his cravat threw two half-crowns at me when I helped him remount. It was a small fortune.

I have a collection of sounds in my brain that are reminders of those times. When they float free, on sleepless nights and black days, they plunge me into a strange mix of pleasure and sadness. I hear the honking of wild geese passing over our house on frosty November evenings. I hear the whirr of mowing machines in early summer. I hear a vixen crying in the dead of night. And always the bugle call at mid-morning and the rising swell of beagle tongue.

Fox-hunting will die. It was dying when I followed the hunt across moor and parkland. The era that supported it, the wealth of great houses and their vast estates, is no more. It was ebbing away in my time. Castles were falling and cabins rising. The Romans had a phrase for it: so pass the glories of the world. I hear these words in ruined manors and broken stonewalls.

★

I always stopped on the bridge over the Deel. It is one of Limerick's main rivers. It rises in the mountain foothills to the west and winds its way through fertile lands until it merges with the sea. I had the idea that one day I would search for the source of the Deel. I never found it because when I started to fish, the thought went out of my head. But I would get to know every turn, swirl and eddy between Rath and miles downstream, far below the weir at New Bridge.

A year or two before, I had found a fishhook stuck in the lapel of my father's jacket. I took the fishhook, cut

and peeled a hazel pole and hooked a
worm to a length of black thread. That
simple action killed my interest in
horses and the fox-hunt. We became
like friends, the Deel and I, wanting
each other's company. The river spoke
to me in song. It read to me from the
book of its landscape, telling me the
secrets of its journey. I was never much
of a fisherman either, because the
whispers and the secrets distracted me.

On summer evenings, when the sun
went down, a group of us used to make
for the Deel. It was said that there was
a depth of ten feet in the middle of
Dore's Hole. It was as black, as my
father would say, as the hobs of hell.
When I rounded the bend, saw the evil
looking sheen on the water surface and
heard the sucking sound as the flow
swirled under the banks, it filled me
with fear. None of us could swim. We

groped around the black hole, lying on sheaves of rushes, arms and legs pumping like a threshing machine. The noise of our pleasure brought more and more youngsters to swell the group.

Then three young women arrived one evening. They stood gaping at us from the bank. The women were older than us, louder and more sure of themselves. They demanded equal rights to the black pool. When we refused and dared them to do something about it, they went behind the bushes and came out in bathing costumes. It was the closest we had come to young female nudity. It stopped us in our tracks. One moment we were full of innocent bravado. The next we were struck dumb with our mouths open in shock.

The women slid down the bank.

Their bathing costumes were pulled out of line. Dark hidden places were revealed. Our eyes had rested on forbidden fruits and the crime of looking, as our priest would later say, was a terrible sin. Then we remembered that we were stark naked beneath the black water. Nothing separated us from the gaze of these young women except a sheaf of rushes. This must have been the way that Adam felt in the Garden of Eden. We pulled our grass skirts around us and went home in silence. A few confessed to the priest and the blame fell on all of us. That black hole was a place of sin and we were ordered not to go there again. Then the rushes grew wild around the rim of the pool. The bushes closed off the way in and no one ever swam in Dore's Hole again.

Sometimes, in heavy rainfall, the

water reached the top of the twin arches. I walked through quickly then because the rush of water scared me. It came round the bend in a great rush after the heavy rains. Branches of trees, dead animals and clumps of earth were carried along in its watery grasp. My mother had a rhyme about a man called Brian O'Linn. He was a kind of simple country hero who made fun of danger. I remembered the same verse every time I went over the bridge, especially when the river was in flood.

Brian O'Linn and his wife and wife's mother,
They all went over the bridge together.
The bridge broke down and they all fell in,
We'll go home by water, said Brian O'Linn.

When the river flooded it spilled onto the road and under the door of

Mick Rock's cottage. He and his family had to move in with his brother until the floods had gone and the dampness dried out. Mick was a short man with wiry white hair and twinkling blue eyes. He was forever about the yard, brushing on lime-wash or leaning on the handle of a spade. Mick would bring me into the kitchen, put the kettle on and question me for news.

After Rock's house I had less knowledge about the places I was travelling in. Sometimes I would meet a man called The Count who had a big house in the dip behind the hill. He used to ask me to bring messages: a pound of sausages, wire, nails, twine. I never got a penny for my trouble. Once he asked me to bring him a ball of wax-end from Brand's saddlery. He told me to leave it in a hole in the wall beside the gatepost. He gave me three pence for the wax-end and a halfpenny for myself. It was a paltry sum, even in those days. Plus I had to wait two hours until Brand decided to serve a country youngster. He must have thought that lads like me had nothing better to do than to wait around. I left the wax-end in a different hiding-place to the one he told me. It eased my anger and made me feel that was I was a match for smart people like The Count and the harness-maker.

I thought about the wax-end twenty years later and went to look for it. By then a great change had swept over my route to Rath. Land had been given back to landlords' tenants. The great houses were falling down. The Count was dead and so was Mick Rock. Not for years had a youngster walked that road bearing messages on a Saturday morning. But the ball of wax-end was still there. It fell apart when I touched it and a lift of breeze carried off its ashes. It was like a burial of all the things that had gone.

★

If I were lucky, and if I had timed my journey well, Miss Daisy would appear shortly. Like myself, she went to town every Saturday but, unlike me, she had transport. She drove a pony and trap — a grey pony the colour of limestone. The pony had two speeds only, slow and dead slow. But it didn't matter. The trap was the height of luxury. There was a rug to place over the knees and the seats had cushions. Even more wonderful was the oilskin cover that fitted into the shape of the seated body. It was fixed to the wood of the backrest with brass studs. It saved the rug from wind and rain and kept the lower body snug and dry. My father's trap cart had none of those frills. When it rained, water ran from the knees down to the floor. A puddle grew that sometimes reached our ankles.

I thought Miss Daisy was the perfect lady, just like the pictures I had seen in my mother's books. I could imagine her seated in an elegant drawing room, taking tea in fine-bone china. The little finger of her right hand would stick out from the others. I pictured her as a woman of proper manners and correct behaviour. But the painted fingernails gave a different image. So too did the face-powder that streaked across her cheekbones as if she had wiped her face with her hands while she baked. Miss Daisy had a very refined way of speaking. She always asked for my mother and father and made small sounds of concern when something was amiss.

'Dear, dear, dear, dear,' she repeated in time to the sounds of concern. If the matter was serious enough, we would say a decade of the rosary. When we were finished, she would say, 'There now, that's grand. God will take care of it.'

Every now and then the pony broke wind. Daisy took it as a personal offence, as if the animal had chosen to embarrass her in front of company.

'You bold boy! You bold, bold boy! Have you no manners at all? We're not alone, you know.'

Most of the women I knew of Daisy's age — probably middle forties — would simply see such things as everyday acts of nature. Breaking wind was regarded as a healthy sign. Some medical men said it was a proper thing to do even in company. My father had that in rhyme from a doctor.

Wherever you be, let the wind break free,
For stopping it caused the death of me.

Miss Daisy got quite upset about language that did not match the gentle ways of her spirit. She gave out to me for using the word 'bloody'. It was common and vulgar, but not nearly as awful as the soldier's word, then doing the rounds.

I should promise her, she pleaded, that such a word would never pass my lips. I told her I didn't know anything about it, which wasn't quite true. Chris Wilmot, a classmate, had used it in the school playground. Miss Abigail had slapped him with the ruler. It was lucky, she said, that he had used the word while he was in the playground. If he had used it indoors, the priest would have had to come and bless the place. It was as bad as that.

'How will I know it when I hear it'? I asked Miss Daisy.

Her features twisted. Particles of rouge seemed to move about her face as her jaw went up and down.

'I hope you never hear it,' she said, 'but in case you do, the word begins with an 'f' and there's a 'k' at the end.' It was on the tip of my tongue to ask her how she had heard it, given the polite world that she lived in.

She also gave out to me for using our local mode of speech. We said mate for meat, crame for cream, hate for heat and so on. It was common, Daisy said, a sign that we were rude and uneducated.

Every time the pony broke wind, Miss Daisy feared the worst. It was a sign that any moment now a load would be dropped into the body of the trap cart. When my father suspected that the pony was about to relieve itself, he put pressure on the tail so that the load would be kept out of the cart. When Miss Daisy tried the same thing, it looked comical and so out of place. Her fingers, with their rings and painted nails, pressed desperately against the tail, and she turned her face away in a look of disgust and horror. She seldom succeeded, because the force of nature was greater than Miss Daisy's hand. We were visited by the full load.

'You bold, bad boy! You bold, bold, bad boy!'

We stopped to clean out. Miss Daisy had a short handled broom under the seat and we brushed the pile through the door at the rear of the trap.

'Promise me now that you won't do that again. Promise now, you hear?'

The pony seemed to nod at the

order and Miss Daisy smiled. If everything held good, she would be home before the pony had the urge again.

We came to a place called the Stony Man. At the crossroads, there had once been a forge. There was a statue of a blacksmith high up in an archway of the front wall. The stone blacksmith, in steel-blue limestone, looked deep in thought. One leg was bent and the point of an elbow was resting on the flat part of the anvil. The Stony Man, as we called it, gazed out forever on stone-walled fields, on dairy herds and half-bred hunters. This was rich and fertile land and had been fought over for hundreds of years.

The Stony Man marked another part of my route to the town. I was now entering places that I knew very little about. The land was better than ours and the farms were bigger. There were two-storeyed slated houses with avenues and lawns and iron gates.

From here, a system of roads circled large tracts owned by the Massey estate. We went, Miss Daisy and I, and the steel-grey pony, in silent respect by the stonewall that enclosed that vast amount of land. We passed the main entrance. On either side were two stone piers. The wall between seemed to be like a raised wing that would at any moment take flight. Such was the angle of the gateway that the main house was not visible from the curious eyes of the people who passed on the road. There was a pair of stone lions on the inner columns, each with a raised foot, watching outwards over the plain. I thought how wonderful it was for some that they could journey through life like the lions, a foot pressed down on the rest of us because we were ordinary people and not noble like those within the gates. When I was on foot, I would peer in through the gates and hope to catch a glimpse of life within the walls. Miss Daisy always pulled up too, but we never saw beyond the gate-lodge.

The winding avenue curved away through the fields, past great beech trees. It lost itself beyond a series of little bends. The children of the gate-lodge played in the dust amid the hens and the bantam fowl and looked just the same as other children on our side of the wall.

We called the people who owned the huge estates the 'quality' because they were seen as far more important than the rest of us. They lived lives that were far removed from our simple ways. But every now and then something would happen that gave us a glimpse of how they lived. We were taking the midday meal on a Sunday when a jeep pulled into the front yard. Out stepped a man wearing baggy pants, a tweed cap and a yellow waistcoat. He and his party were going to shoot snipe in the marshy field at the end of our avenue. He asked if some of us children would come down, beat the grass and drive out the snipe.

Four of us went. We walked into a scene that was more likely to be found in upper-class England. A fleet of expensive motorcars had parked on the edge of the white road. Women sat on shooting sticks with tartan rugs over their knees. They waited to be served lunch by the butler and his assistant. Great baskets of food were laid on the ground. Men were opening wine bottles or standing around in small groups. Their white-gloved hands were twirling silver-topped walking sticks. They could have been at the Ascot races or strolling through a London park on a summer day.

We flushed out the snipe. The shooters brought them down as the birds flew over the white road. Some of the women were better shots than their men. We beat the bogland a couple of times because the snipe that had lived through the first shots returned in their fright to the marsh again. The butler and his assistant collected the fallen snipe and counted them in pairs. He entered the number in a red notebook and gave it to the man driving the jeep.

The butler threw all the snipe into a canvas bag and presented it to my elder brother. And then there followed a wonderful thing. The butler put his uniform cap on the ground. One by one they came — the major and his lady, the colonel and the master of hounds that I had seen before, men who owned coal mines and factories. They tossed coins into the cap: half-crowns and florins and the odd shilling piece. We thought we would never be poor again.

I wanted to hide the money in the loft in the outhouse where no one ever went. I had never seen so much in my life. We were still standing there after the shooting party had gone. The sun broke through a cloud and a single ray found its way to the money in the uniform cap. It was only then I became aware that the butler had forgotten to take it.

'Don't worry,' my brother John said, 'there's plenty more caps where that came from.'

I told him that I had plans for the money. Every Saturday, when I was going to shop in Rath, I would bring some, just a little, and buy oranges and chocolate and other wonderful things that my older sisters were always on about. But he claimed that he had more power than I had because he was a year older. We would bring the money home, give it to my mother and watch the way her face lit up in surprise and wonder.

It happened just the way he said it would. For a little while she said nothing. She just stood there with her lips pressed together as if she was doubting what she saw with her own eyes. Then her eyes lit up. She grabbed my brother and swirled him around the kitchen, doing a dance. Then she put the money into the secret drawer in the press beside the fire. We all knew that it was there but we were afraid to go near it as if it were some kind of holy place.

I never got a six-penny bit to take to the town in Rath and buy a bar of chocolate. When I asked my mother she shook her head and pressed her lips together again. This time there was no light in her eyes, only a touch of sadness.

'I was going to buy a dress,' she told me, 'but something else came up that was more important.'

That was the story of her life. Every time she scraped together a little money to buy something for herself, another matter had to be taken care of.

*

Far in beyond the gates and over the top of the lime trees around the great house, we could see the tops of the chimney pots. It was from estates like this one that the high-ranking soldiers of the Empire came. Every son behind those walls, except the one who was going to inherit the land, would be sent off to a boarding school in England soon after his tenth birthday. My father used to tell me stories about such things and they kept me awake at night. The young lads that were sent away were no older than I was then. I thought it was cruel and heartless to send them away at that age. But my father only shook his head when I said that to him.

'That's the way of the quality,' he said

One windy, rainy day as I returned from Rath, a Bentley motorcar purred up beside me. I was just opposite one of the old workhouses on the outskirts of Rath. The driver pushed open the door on the passenger side and told me he would take me to the gates of Stoneville, near The Stony Man. The moment he closed the door, I was in a seat of comfort and wealth. I could see the reflection of my face in the walnut wood that was set into the dashboard and around the doorframes. It was the most luxurious seat I had ever sat in. I could smell polish from the leather and hear a faint creak when the car moved forward. I felt I was riding high on the saddle of a hunting horse.

The driver spoke with an accent I had never heard before. I found it hard to make out the words. They seemed to spin around in his mouth like pebbles and then slide through his lips as though covered in treacle. By that time I was in my first year at boarding school. When I told him that I was studying Latin and Greek, his face lit up. He asked me for my name. It was Greek, he told me. There was a famous man called Nestor, whom Homer had written about. He was a king and had a palace at a place called Pylos. For a long time they thought that Pylos was just a story but the palace had lately been found after being buried for over three thousand years. This man, Nestor, he told me, was known far and wide for his wisdom. When we came to Stoneville, he drove straight by, out past the Stony Man and across the bridge over the Deel. He had been to Greece and had seen the places we learned about at school.

He left me out at the crossroads beyond the river telling me that he was going to Alta, another great house. He was sorry he couldn't talk further with me. Perhaps we might meet again. I went towards home and when I looked around, he had turned the car and was heading back in the other direction. He wasn't going to Alta at all. I wondered why he should tell a fib about it and why he had brought me much farther than his own place. Maybe he thought he was doing a good deed for a young lad who reminded him of his own childhood. He was the truth of my father's story, sent off to a boarding school in far away England when he was much younger than me. He hated every moment of it, he told me. The loneliness was worst of all.

We never met again.

★

We journeyed on, Miss Daisy and I, along the length of the stonewall and the over-hanging trees. Horses grazed in the fields. Yearlings played in the shelter of the beech tress. Herds of fine cattle stood still and munched. We came then to the marvel of science that was closing the doors on a dark past.

Ten years before electric power had come to Rath. It would have the most important effect on rural Ireland, though it would be many years before electricity came to the house where I lived. Nothing changed our lives like the 'electric' did, even if, in the beginning, it was just another way of lighting our houses. In time it was the power that worked the radio. It cooked our meals, milked the cows, warmed our houses and brought us into the twentieth century.

Beside the crossroad there was a new powerhouse. I thought it looked like a space-age station. Wires were fixed to the walls and ran along in a strange pattern. There was a set of glass disks, like upturned cups, connected to the wires or sitting on top of cross-shaped arms that jutted out from the building. But it was the hum, like an ever-present throb, which amazed me the most. It was like another language that only people from a far away planet could understand. The hum pulsed and flowed and when I closed my eyes. It made me feel that I was a time traveller in a spaceship.

When I was alone, I stopped and listened for that hum. It both scared and excited me. There was a host of stories about the electric. They always happened when something new came along which people didn't understand. Some of the stories were true, some complete nonsense. All around the powerhouse there were signs warning about the dangers within and without. But the ever-present hum took hold of my curiosity and filled me with a desire to know more about it. Around where that powerhouse stood, little had changed in two centuries. The horse was still king; men worked the land without the aid of modern machines.

I remember thinking about those things again, seven years later, when I got off the train after an interview for a job in Shannon Airport. My father was waiting, holding the pony by the head, because the hiss of steam would scare it. He was talking to Julius, whose ancestors had come out of Germany. They had brought with them the long-faced spade, the idea of planting in drills, the craft of grafting fruit trees and growing cabbages.

Not so long ago, the horse-drawn mowing machine had come on the scene. It would be obsolete in a few years. And as it passed it would take the draft-horse, the long-faced spade and the making of hay trams. A great change was sweeping the land. I had come that day from a place where aircraft landed and men spoke different languages. But those two men, my father and old Julius, who had come from different ways of life, were as alike now as peas in a pod. I watched old Julius with his wagging finger and serious looking face, my father nodding. Neither of them had yet heard the hum of change. Nor would they hear it if they were asked to listen.

The railway passed under the bridge where the sprawl of town houses began. The railway is gone now, and a new roundabout diverts the traffic away from the station house. My mother loved travelling by train. Sometimes she brought me with her. We took the pony and trap to the railway station and once out of sight of the house, my mother's face brightened. She sang snatches of song and her feet tapped to its rhythm. At the station, old Julius appeared out of nowhere, raised his cap, and took the pony from the trap. When my mother entered the carriage, such a change came over her that I thought I was seeing a different woman. Now she was visiting those places she had imagined through her reading. She was travelling in a foreign country, going to strange, out of the ordinary places.

The carriages were wood-panelled. There were pictures of great houses and beautiful scenes fixed to the panels. She studied them closely and read the titles aloud. Then she sat, leaned back, and closed her eyes. The beginnings of a smile crept from the corners of her mouth and spread like a warming glow across her face. I thought again how beautiful she looked.

The steam engine was the fastest

form of travel we were yet aware of. My father never shared my mother's love of rail travel because he had a dread of what he called 'unholy speed'. There was no need in his world for such mad disregard for life and limb. His neighbours would have agreed. I got a lift once from John Lynch and his grandfather in their ass and cart. When we passed the hurling field, a train came around the bend. Though it was slowing for the station, the young lad's face was alive with excitement.

'There's speed for you,' he kept saying. 'Boys, that's speed.'

The old man had his hand over his eyes.

Miss Daisy and I drove into Ward's yard. We removed the pony from the trap cart and took off most of the harness. There was a sack filled with hay under the seat. We fixed it over the pony's head and led him to a hitching post.

She never offered me a lift home and I often wondered about it until late one evening I wandered into the snug of Culhane's pub. There I saw Miss Daisy and another lady with tumblers of whiskey in front of them. Miss Daisy was smoking a cigarette from a Craven A packet. There was a half-inch of ash dangling from its end. She had a grin that made her face look crooked. In her eyes was a watery glint, as if the cold had made them stream. When she saw me she gathered herself, sat erect and waved me away with an angry shake of her hand.

Miss Daisy never passed me on the road again. I met her once in Brand's when I was getting a message for The Count. She told me that she now came a different route. The lower road, as she called it, was shorter and quicker. I had walked both ways several times and knew that she was mistaken.

OPEN DOOR SERIES

Driving With Daisy by Tom Nestor

It All Adds Up by Margaret Neylon

Has Anyone Here Seen Larry?
by Deirdre Purcell

<u>SERIES FOUR</u>

Fair-Weather Friend by Patricia Scanlan

The Story of Joe Brown by Rose Doyle

The Smoking Room by Julie Parsons

World Cup Diary by Niall Quinn

The Quiz Master by Michael Scott

Stray Dog by Gareth O'Callaghan

ORDER DETAILS OVERLEAF

TRADE/CREDIT CARD ORDERS TO:
CMD, 55A Spruce Avenue,
Stillorgan Industrial Park,
Blackrock, Co Dublin, Ireland.
Tel: (+353 1) 294 2560
Fax: (+353 1) 294 2564

TO PLACE PERSONAL/EDUCATIONAL
ORDERS OR TO ORDER A CATALOGUE
PLEASE CONTACT:
New Island, 2 Brookside, Dundrum
Road, Dundrum, Dublin 14, Ireland.
Tel: (+353 1) 298 6867/298 3411
Fax: (+353 1) 298 7912
website www.newisland.ie